Fragments of Time

Emily Smith

BookLeaf Publishing

India | USA | UK

Presentation by *BookLeaf Publishing*

Web: www.bookleafpub.com

E-mail: info@bookleafpub.com

ISBN: 9789363313170

First edition 2025

*I dedicate this book to myself for seeing a spark
ignite and running with it as far as it will glow.*

ACKNOWLEDGMENT

I would like to acknowledge and thank everyone who has reached out to me and let me know they could see themselves in my poetry and relate to the emotions within those words.

PREFACE

This book of poems leans heavily into my search for understanding and meaning in the daily struggles that stay with us and weigh us down.

Dirt

There are days I don't want to be here,
And by here, I mean planet Earth.
Those days, I would give anything,
To be returned to nothing but dirt.

I'd like to be a pebble on the shoreline,
A leaf dancing in the breeze,
A puddle after a rainstorm,
Or a feather that floats with ease.

Something without a heartbeat,
Something that cannot be seen,
A sound that comes as a whisper,
Gliding gently through the trees.

Something that does not feel,
Something that cannot taste,
Unaware of human distractions,
Knows nothing of consumption and waste.

I want to be free of life's burdens,
Free of stress, frustration, and guilt.
I want comfort that does not come unraveled,
Like the seams of a time-honored quilt.

To be free like the waves on the ocean,
Or the droplets that come down as rain,
That settles and soaks into the earth,
I want to be dirt again.

Meaning

I need a feeling in my stomach,
A pounding in my chest.
I need a joy that fills my heart,
Giving me a reason to suggest,

That my body belongs amidst,
The beings that are already here,
To add to the chaos and pleasure,
That humans both love and fear.

A reason to keep getting up,
A reason to move through the dark,
A reason to smile and laugh and care,
A reason to embark.

On new and foreign journeys,
To travel in and out,
To whisper to each season,
"I know, I have my doubts."

But I've been told that it's all worth it,
The pain, in the very end.
Worth the heartbreak and the torment,
The loss of family and friends.

I've worked my fingers to the bone,
I strive to do my best,
I give as much as I possibly can,
What I really need is rest.

Rest to find my purpose here,
To find the depths within my soul.
Rest to recharge and ignite my magic,
To help show me my worldly role.

I need to know what I'm doing here,
Sometimes I just don't understand,
Just what the meaning is for me,
Why my feet have graced this land.

Why my words have strength and meaning,
Where my being is of service,
What my time can offer life's movement,
Who can tell me of my purpose?

I haven't found that special spot,
Where I feel a motive for my being.
I'm still searching for the answers,
For life to have some meaning.

Maybe It's Me

Maybe it's me who's different,
Maybe it's me who's changed.
Maybe it's taking me so long to heal,
Because I haven't pulled out my fangs.

I've kept my fangs inside this time,
I did not reveal them to protect my heart,
I let you have the whole damn thing,
And my heart you tore apart.

I permitted myself to open up,
Gave my emotions a chance to fly,
And you clipped my wings and let me fall,
While I was flying high.

I believed in this heightened feeling
Of trust and security,
Not realizing that you weren't real,
You were playing games with me.

Now I lie here injured,
My wounds, an open book,
For others to come and peek inside,
And witness what you took.

My love, my joy, my excitement, my time,
I thought the feelings shared were true.
I will find a way to keep my heart open,
And not close it because of you.

Open Sea

See, the truth is, the word Love
Does not have to be spoken,
In order for the heart,
To crack and become broken.

Break from the words
That fell from your lips,
Words that could crumble mountains,
Words that could sink ships.

Words of no longer, words of conclusion,
Words that signal the end.
Words that cancel budding growth,
Words that broke, they did not bend.

I can see us there, in that space that once was,
For I just cannot see us any other way,
My memories, constantly pulling me back,
To the feelings that took hold that day.

A feeling so special and pure,
A feeling I thought would never come for me.
Now with that feeling gone again,
I float, drifting in an open sea.

A sea of what ifs, a sea of whens,
A sea of will it ever be.
A sea so dark, so cold, so deep,
I'm afraid I may never be seen.

That's where I'm at; it's dark, it's cold,
I cannot see beneath my feet.
But I bob and tread and stay afloat,
Until these tired, swimming legs take a seat.

My heart hurts in a regular way,
On a very daily basis.
My only opportunity for a break,
Is my dreamlike state of oasis.

If I can dream it, I can see it,
And that is just what I need,
A heart so big, so brave, so strong,
It keeps beating until it's received.

My Journey

My journey hasn't exactly been
A trip I would have planned for myself.
I've walked down alleys I'd never wish
Upon anybody else.

I've faced moments so appalling,
It felt like I must be in hell.
I've drawn myself inward so tightly,
You can now only see my shell.

There are little moments,
So dark and so cold,
They would scare right away,
The strong, brave, and bold.

I've tried to keep my chin up,
My mind open, my heart clear,
But the fog of disappointment,
Tends to dampen and destroy my cheer.

I can't foresee the future,
I know not what it will hold,
But the present feels so empty,
This lonely life feels cold.

There are no arms to wrap me in
When I am sad or scared.
There are no ears to listen,
When my feelings have been snared.

There are no comforting words,
To heal an aching soul.
No hands to hold when times get hard,
To remind you that you're whole.

No evenings of enchantment,
Set beneath the stars.
No soft and gentle kisses,
To help heal all the scars.

I'm trying to feel content,
Amidst this growing, burning need,
To walk this path with someone else,
Where my heart beats at double speed.

What Went Wrong?

Why was it too much?
What made me feel that way?
Now whenever I see you,
I don't know what to say.

I don't know where to begin,
But my heart and mind want to speak.
The words get jumbled in my throat,
My sentence structure becomes weak.

I ruined it; it's all my fault,
I clipped our flying wings.
My actions were wrong, my words were worse,
I don't blame you for a thing.

I know my memory only brings to the top,
The good things that I'm searching for now.
But why couldn't I appreciate you,
When I had you, your gifts I wouldn't allow.

I remember the things we wanted,
Were never, ever the same.
I remember the futures we dreamed of,
In different directions, they came.

I try to think of the bad times,
When I happen upon your face.
But it's only good that comes to the surface,
The bad times gone without a trace.

You weren't mean; you weren't nasty,
You just weren't the one for me.
But right now our never future,
Is the only thing I can see.

The once was, now forgotten,
The used to, now gone.
The forever now lost between us,
I'll never understand what went wrong.

Not Enough

It was really nice to see you,
It's been so very long.
I'll smile and keep on walking,
Reminding myself to be strong.

I must remember how much you needed,
And I just couldn't give my time.
I bring back to recollection,
How hard I struggled to shine.

It comes to mind how I felt,
When I first disliked your scent.
And how much I knew right then and there,
Our time together was spent.

Those feels I had when we first met,
Have since lost their touch.
But I think about it often,
And often is too much.

I'm so sorry it wasn't enough for me,
It turns out I needed more.
You had the world to offer,
It cut me to the core.

So now I search the world again,
For those things you offered me.
Why weren't you enough?
Why couldn't I let things be?

Cruel

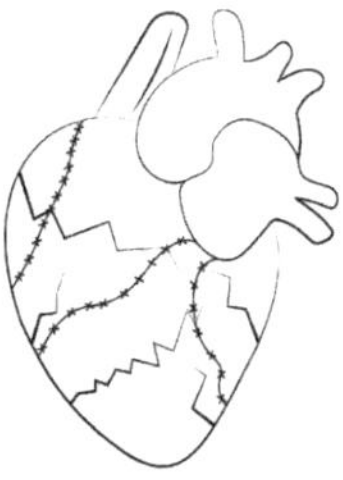

The world is cruel,
It's an unkind space.
With knives in the spot
Where fingers are placed.

Knives that cut deep as they
Hold you down here.
Piercing the skin
And creating deep fear,

Of tense earthly pressures
That cannot be avoided.
Of the cracks in existence
That make us disjointed.

The sour, bitter taste of
Experience and regret,
Memories tainted by disdain,
That we cannot forget.

Our time playing back in our minds
Like a movie.
Many moments taking pause,
As the memory runs through me.

Not pleasure, but pain,
That I've still not let go.
Because the world is such a cruel place,
Didn't you know?

Thankful

I should be thankful
That I still exist here,
That my parts continue moving,
Through doubt and through fear.

I should be thankful
For the things that I have,
Those things I have worked for,
How I've moved up the graph.

I should be thankful,
For all the lessons I've learned,
For mistakes I keep making,
For the answers I've earned.

I should be thankful
For the experiences I've shared.
The adventures I've gone on,
With people who cared.

I should be thankful
For all of the people I've known.
Who've helped guide and prepare me
For the amazing places I'll go.

I should be thankful
For all that I've got,
But when I weigh it all out,
I'm afraid that I'm not.

Sold a Story

We've been sold a story
That we can walk through walls,
The world will offer up for us,
That we can have it all.

But we've been sold a story,
A book that has an end,
A fantasy with no future,
A friendship with no friend.

A book that's full of pages,
With words that don't make sense.
We sit there in our garden,
Surrounded by a fence.

A fence that keeps us stagnant,
A fence that keeps us still,
Allows no forward movement,
Degrades color, strength, and will.

We smile as we listen
To the story read aloud,
Our dreams float to the surface,
With the ease of a soft cloud.

But then the tale is over,
And the storybook is closed,
The words still float around me,
While a new feeling slowly grows.

These tales we've been told,
That grow slowly in our mind,
Are difficult to follow,
And so very hard to find.

Those stories will take us there,
To that little fantasy life.
But we'll still have to wake up,
We'll still have to open our eyes.

Anxiety

My anxiety has the floor today,
It's calling all the shots.
Keeping sanity at bay,
And tying my stomach up in knots.

Do you remember that thing you said,
That thing you did, that dress you wore?
How you wished you'd disappear,
Or just blend right in with the floor.

What did they see, what did they think,
What did they hear, what did they say?
Oh, how I felt like such a huge
Embarrassment that day.

To play that awkward record of events,
On repeat inside my head.
Thinking if only the earth could open up,
And swallow me down and dead.

To be free of constant worry, constant fear,
And constant dread.
The more it keeps on going,
The more it keeps it fed.

What if? What if? What if?
It never does shut down.
Drives me round and round in circles,
Like a toy car with its clown.

Mind spinning in spirals,
Heart racing the track,
Sweat beads all over my body,
Like highways traverse a map.

Deep breaths to calm it down,
Count to ten and hold it in.
Fresh air and a quiet space,
To make me feel human again.

Empty

Sometimes it's so hard
To move about your day.
Every second is a chore,
In every single way.

Don't want to see, don't want to hear,
Don't want to think, don't want to be.
Don't want to do a God Damn thing,
And definitely don't want to be me.

It feels too much, it feels too heavy,
Every moment a ton of bricks.
Life delivering its vengeance and anger,
With its big ole' bag of tricks.

This must be what it feels like
When drowning in quicksand.
The harder you try to get free,
The more impossible it is to stand.

It's just going through the motions,
Just trying to get things done.
Because I have to, because I must,
Not for enjoyment or pleasure or fun.

I'm thankful and grateful for the things that I
have,
But somehow I'm not happy at all.
There are moments of sunshine sprinkled
throughout,
But most days I just wait for the fall.

Still Unsolved

I was never yours,
And you were never mine,
We just happened to come together,
At this special place and time.

For just a little moment,
We entered each other's lives,
Creating memories for our timeline,
Before we ended with goodbyes.

I was ready for big things,
I was ready for a change.
I saw a door open up for me,
It felt new, exciting, and strange.

I was a strong and confident woman,
And you were just but a boy.
I thought I'd found the love of my life,
While you had found a new toy.

I had big dreams of a future,
Where visions of intimacy evolved.
Now just a dot in the background
Of a narrative, still unsolved.

Future Dreams

My dreams for the future
Are not crazy, they're not wild.
They are simple things, really,
You could even say they're mild.

I have a house, I have a car,
I've worked hard in my career.
I have traveled and seen great things,
But there's more to life, I fear.

I'm proud of my achievements,
Confident in my abilities,
Honored to be a part of lives not mine,
Yet there's still something more, it seems.

It's not the same for everyone,
We don't all search for the same things,
But there is something in this life for us,
That just might give me wings.

Someone to call my own,
A love that's just for me,
An endless sea of beauty,
That puts my panic at ease.

A gentle kiss to say hello,
A soft touch to wrap me in,
A little look to know you're mine,
And that you're ready to begin.

A brand new life with me,
A life that's yours and mine and ours.
Where we can waste away our days,
As we weather life's rain showers.

It seems that a little piece is missing,
This life of me and you.
But in these future visions of mine,
All my dreams come true.

Childhood

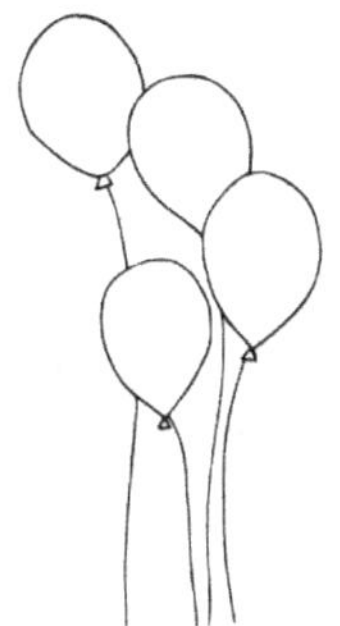

I miss childhood,
And daytime birthday parties.
Opening presents, eating cake,
Then playing with our Barbies.

Going home with a friend
With a bus pass after school,
Riding bikes, eating ice cream,
Spending summer days at the pool.

Getting dropped off at the mall,
To walk around and socialize.
Spend our money at the movies,
Then get an Olga and some fries.

Next thing you know, we're driving in our car,
Riding up and down the strip,
Seeing friends and making new ones,
Man, the 90's were a trip!

Then it's after-school jobs, prom,
All-night parties, and graduation.
It seems so long, and then so short,
And then, just memories to take from.

I miss childhood,
And all those innocent moments,
Having open, boundless freedom,
Before we all became grown-ups.

Hands

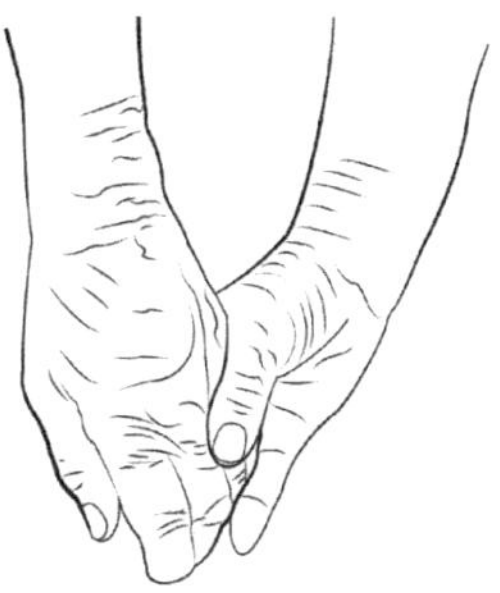

I see it in my hands,
They do not look the same,
The cracks and bumps and wrinkles,
My eyes have watched them change.

Over the course of many years,
I didn't even know it,
Time moves so very fast,
You cannot grab or hold it.

They used to be so gentle,
Feminine and soft.
That youthful look is gone now,
The vibrancy is lost.

These hands have weathered time,
Over forty years they've seen.
They've been so many places,
A tactile extension of me.

These hands have lifted weights, hammered
nails,
Drilled holes and baked a million cakes.
They've painted pictures, torn up paper,
Oared a boat down a peaceful lake.

These hands have punched, squeezed, caressed,
Written more words than a novel could hold.
They've dribbled a ball, driven a car,
They've held hands, sad and cold.

These hands have built furniture,
More than that, they've built this entire life.
These hands have been moving,
Since before they came alive.

These hands are strong and tender,
These hands are kind and rough,
These hands are aging with me,
These hands of mine are just enough.

Goodnight

We never said goodbye,
We always said goodnight.
That's why a light still lingers there,
With hope to reignite.

That beautiful, glowing brightness,
For a moment lit up my world,
Spoiled the child inside me,
Found that innocent little girl.

The one with hopes and dreams
That had never once been squashed.
Endless possibilities ahead of her,
Not yet soiled, broken, and washed.

When ideas were energetic,
Not silly or unrealistic.
When the open road ahead,
Held prospects, both intriguing and mystic.

Instead of carrying the incredible weight
Of society's gross opinion.
And afraid that others could topple,
My great and powerful dominion.

Now I'm trying so very hard,
To be happy, but it feels so wrong.
I was doing so well at this,
Until you came along.

It's the goodnight that keeps me going,
I remember the sound so well.
The last time we hung up the phone,
Goodnight is where I dwell.

Fragments of Time

Fragments of stolen time,
That's all I'd get from you.
A minute here, a second there,
And I was content with it too.

Just to still be with you,
Share those moments by your side.
Feel the safety and security,
I've searched for, all this time.

I wouldn't pull, I wouldn't push,
I wouldn't demand a single thing.
I was not at all possessive,
So you couldn't hear me sing.

Not because I wasn't,
But because you failed to hear.
I was singing the whole time,
You couldn't hear me now, I fear.

You were wrapped up in yourself,
In your wants and aches and needs.
I fit your space, just for a second,
Then you wanted me to leave.

That's ok, I won't stay,
I don't need to be where I'm not wanted.
Those wants and needs of mine,
Now I hope they keep you haunted.

Healing

I'm working on healing,
But I'm not fully healed.
Like an orange or banana,
There are layers to be peeled.

Complex skins of pain and joy,
For decades carried upon shoulders,
Weighing down triumph and internal peace,
Putting obstacles on the path like boulders.

Another scar, another strike,
At times worn so proud,
Now I need to calm and soothe them,
Because their effects are much too loud.

For too long center stage
Has been the destination for character fear.
Masked by yelling and anger,
Letting rage drive and steer.

Clarity only now,
In the calm of the storm,
When my fists are tired,
And my muscles forlorn.

From tensing and holding
The anger inside,
Not allowing the tears
To override my pride.

Slowly but steadily,
I strip it all off,
The words and the actions
That created the thoughts.

That dance in my head
From sun up to sun down,
Sometimes I float,
Sometimes I drown.

Each layer reveals a
New price within,
A feeling that signals
Fight or flight to begin.

I'm working on healing
I'm not finished yet.
I'm not even swimming,
I've just gotten my feet wet.

Lost Cause

This fantasy I have,
It's time to let it go.
Security, safety, and love
Are just things I'll never know.

I'll know it from the perspective
Of family and friends.
But not something I'll receive
From a man again.

I hate to voice this out loud,
But partnerships aren't for me.
The universe has decidedly shown,
It's something it doesn't want me to see.

The happiness it gives to others,
Was chosen only for them.
My happiness must come from different things,
It shall never come from men.

Men are selfish and evil,
And vile and mean.
Men do cruel and awful things,
The majority of which you've never seen.

Consider yourself lucky if you've been chosen
To live inside that precious little box.
Where life doesn't come to visit you,
With hard lessons and jolting shocks.

Beaten down to the point
Of open fissures and breaks,
The universe trips you again,
Just to see how much you can take.

Eventually you surrender,
To the broken, beating heart.
You let it go, still and silent
And you let things fall apart.

No fleet to come running,
With repairs of string and tape.
For the emptiness in these hollow walls,
There is no quick escape.

It's a day of never-ending sorrow,
Under veils of darkness and pain.
As you sink into the nerves,
And the emotional wreckage again.

Reminding yourself you're foolish,
For believing that hopes and dreams,
Were things that you could manifest,
But desire's a lost cause, it seems.

Your Garden

Your focus, so strong,
On what others believe,
Is the key to success
And the life that you need.

But the life that you need
Can only be designed by you.
What fills your heart?
And makes dreams come true?

It's listening to intuition,
Feeling your internal spirit rise,
Let your heart do the talking,
Your aura triples in size.

You're magnetic when you live
The life that's set in your bones.
Unlock the power within you,
Control this life you own.

Walk by the table of expectations,
Run past the wall of doubt,
Scream into the deep, dark void;
"I will not go without!"

You'll have the things meant for you,
They will not pass you by.
The sea of gratitude and fortune
Are taking you on a ride.

We're driving past the things you want,
But only you feel the things you need.
When growing the garden of your dreams,
You have to let go of the weeds.

The weeds are things that hold you back,
They don't let the sunlight in.
Get down on your knees and pull the weeds out,
And your garden can bloom once again.

Time

Time has been stealing from you,
For your entire life.
Slicing up your months and years,
With the sharp blade of a knife.

Time will take your youth,
A child is gone too soon.
Quickly taken by jobs and bills,
No longer dreaming of the moon.

Time will take your looks,
Your skin, no longer bright.
Wrinkles line your hands and face,
Only hidden in dark night.

Time will take your joy,
Slowly your smile fades.
The happiness you once knew,
Has been darkened by life's shades.

Time will take your strength,
Your muscles, softer by the day.
Never realizing in your twenties,
That you'd ever feel this way.

Time takes your motivation,
All the things you said you'd do.
With so many days behind us,
Countless dreams are out of view.

But time can also bring us things,
It doesn't only take away.
Time moves fast, and it is fleeting,
But time has given us today.

Time has brought patience,
It has brought understanding.
It's brought friendships and values,
And has kept me freestanding.

I'm thankful for time,
And at the same time, I'm scared,
There are still so many days,
When I feel incredibly unprepared.

But time has also given me,
The gift of thought and knowledge.
Not just because I went to school,
And graduated from college.

The experience that time has given,
Is the most beneficial gift of all.
To look back on and draw upon,
A life that's far from small.

Time will give, and time will take,
With each rotation of the sun.
Time rolls on and gains momentum,
Time creates what we've become.

Friendship

I have made new friends,
Others, I've let go.
Not because I wanted to,
They're just people, I no longer know.

They were not a part,
Of the struggles I went through.
They weren't there to ask,
So they just never knew,

How hard I fought in trying times,
To grow and find myself.
They can only remember me,
As if I were somebody else.

I've tried in many different ways,
To hold space and let them in.
But sometimes life gets busy,
Too busy to be a friend.

We grow, we change, we fluctuate,
On who we are and who we'll be.
I know I've changed a million times,
Trying to discover the real me.

Friendships come and go,
As people constantly change.
True friends will let you discover you,
They'll even help you rearrange.

They're there for you, to cheer you on,
They help you up when you fall down.
They dust you off and hold the mirror,
While you adjust your crown.

Like any other connection,
A friendship can often get lost,
Sometimes the price of keeping them,
Is far too high a cost.

But reflections of that friendship,
Always bring a smile to my face.
For that special friend connection,
My memory forever holds a place.

Forever Sleep

I held you today, cradled in my arms
Together we left home.
When I returned, I walked through the door,
Empty and alone.

Your tiny feet, once running wild,
Up and down the stairs.
Are echos now, but I still see you,
Almost everywhere.

I can't believe you're gone,
My eyes still search for you.
When I look up at the sky,
And see all those shades of blue,

I know that you are up there,
Nestled within the clouds so deep.
Your gentle goodbye tucks you in,
For your forever sleep.

Unburdened

In dreams, I'll close my eyes
And pretend I'm no longer here.
No two feet upon the ground,
Drowning in pain, sorrow, and fear.

Upon soft feathers,
I glide across the sky,
Envisioning a life of beauty
Never seen by human eyes.

Filled with happiness and love,
A joy I simply cannot explain,
Where safety spreads like a rainbow,
After a long and heavy rain.

Unburdened by the weight of humanity,
The judgment of expectation.
The ability to voice my thoughts,
Without the need for explanation.

Drifting into waves of satisfaction,
And out of waves of suspicion.
Finding peace folded into lucidity,
Breaking ties with indecision.

Coasting on the edge of contentment,
No longer seeking to find more.
Finding pleasure in simple surprises,
Empowered to spread my wings and soar.